Biblical Foundation 10

God's Perspective on Finances

D0003130

by Larry Kreider

HOUSE TO HOUSE
PUBLICATIONS

House To House Publications
Ephrata, Pennsylvania USA

God's Perspective on Finances

Larry Kreider

Updated Edition © 2002, Reprinted 2003
Copyright © 1993, 1997, 1999
House to House Publications
1924 West Main Street, Ephrata, PA 17522
Telephone: (717) 738-3751
FAX: (717) 738-0656
Web site: www.dcfi.org

ISBN 1-886973-09-1
Design and illustrations by Sarah Mohler

CONTENTS

Books in this Series

This is the tenth book in a twelve-book series designed to help believers to build a solid biblical foundation in their lives.

A corresponding *Biblical Foundations for Children* book is also available (see page 63).

Introduction

The foundation of the Christian faith is built on Jesus Christ and His Word to us, the Holy Bible. This twelve-book *Biblical Foundation Series* includes elementary principles every Christian needs to help lay a strong spiritual foundation in his or her life.

In this tenth Biblical Foundation book, *God's Perspective on Finances,* we learn that God wants to bless us financially! God desires to meet our needs and provide abundantly for us to minister to others. We will learn that the tithe is a numerical expression reminding us that all we have belongs to God. We are merely managers of the material goods we possess. Scripture has a tremendous amount to say about money or material possessions. Money is such an important issue because a person's attitude toward it often is revealing of his relationship with God. God wants to restore a healthy, godly understanding of finances in the body of Christ today.

In this book, the foundation truths from the Word of God are presented with modern day parables that help you easily understand the basics of Christianity. Use this book and the other 11 *Biblical Foundation* books to lay a solid spiritual foundation in your life, or if you are already a mature Christian, these books are great tools to assist you in discipling others. May His Word become life to you today.

God bless you!
Larry Kreider

How to Use This Resource

Personal study

Read from start to finish as an individual study program to build a firm Christian foundation and develop spiritual maturity.

- Each chapter has a key verse excellent to commit to memory.
- Additional scriptures in gray boxes are used for further study.
- Each reading includes questions for personal reflection and room to journal at the end of the book.

Daily devotional

Use as a devotional for a daily study of God's Word.

- Each chapter is divided into 7-day sections for weekly use.
- Additional days at the end of the book bring the total number of devotionals to one complete month. The complete set of 12 books gives one year's worth of daily devotionals.
- Additional scriptures are used for further study.
- Each day includes reflection questions and a place to write answers at the end of the book.

Mentoring relationship

Use for a spiritual parenting relationship to study, pray and discuss life applications together.

- A spiritual father or mother can easily take a spiritual son or daughter through these short Bible study lessons and use the reflection questions to provoke dialogue about what is learned.
- Read each day or an entire chapter at a time.

Small group study

Study this important biblical foundation in a small group setting.

- The teacher studies the material in the chapters and teaches, using the user-friendly outline provided at the end of the book.

Taught as a biblical foundation course

These teachings can be taught by a pastor or other Christian leader as a basic biblical foundation course.

- Students read an assigned portion of the material.
- In the class, the leader teaches the assigned material using the chapter outlines at the end of the book.

CHAPTER 1

We are Managers of God's Money

KEY MEMORY VERSE

Let a man so consider us, as servants of
Christ and stewards of the mysteries of God.
Moreover it is required in stewards
that one be found faithful.
1 Corinthians 4:1-2 NKJ

God loves a cheerful giver

God wants to bless us financially! John 3:16 says that "God so loved the world that He *gave...*" God introduced Himself to Abraham in Genesis 17 as *El Shaddai*...the God of *more than enough*. He met Abraham's needs and provided abundantly for Abraham to bless the nations. God desires to meet our needs and provide abundantly for us to minister to others.

Many Christians have an unhealthy understanding of finances. They may give out of a sense of duty or obligation. Giving should come out of a sense of faith in God's grace (2 Corinthians 8:1-4); it should never be done grudgingly or out of a sense of compulsion. *Each man should give what he has decided in his heart to give, not reluctantly or under compulsion, for God loves a cheerful giver (2 Corinthians 9:7).* A Christian friend of mine visited a non-believing friend one weekend and asked his friend to attend church with him. My friend recalls how embarrassed he was when he realized the purpose of the service that Sunday morning was to collect money to purchase a new organ. They began to ask for pledges—thousand dollar pledges, five-hundred dollar pledges, and one-hundred dollar pledges. In fact, it took the entire meeting to prod and beg the people to make pledges. The non-Christian friend was so disillusioned by what he experienced, he never wanted to return to church!

Scripture has a tremendous amount to say about money or material possessions. Sixteen of the thirty-eight parables of Jesus deal with money. One out of every ten verses in the New Testament address this subject. Scripture has 500 verses on prayer, less than 500 verses on faith, but over 2,000 verses on the subject of money and material possessions. Money is such an important issue because a person's attitude toward it often is revealing of his relationship with God.

REFLECTION
Why does God want to bless us financially? What should be our attitude in giving?

God wants to restore a healthy, godly understanding of finances in the body of Christ today. Let's be open to what God's Word says about finances.

We are managers only

First and foremost, we must realize that everything we have belongs to God. We are merely stewards (managers) of any material goods we possess. God owns everything we have, but He makes us managers of it. *Let a man so consider us, as servants of Christ and stewards of the mysteries of God. Moreover it is required in stewards that one be found faithful. And what do you have that you did not receive...? (1 Corinthians 4:1-2,7b NKJ).*

When my wife, LaVerne, and I served as missionaries, we had the job of buying the food and supplies for the other missionaries at our base each week. The money we were using was not our own; we were simply managing it. It belonged to the mission board.

I shared this principle of being a manager of God's money in Nairobi, Kenya, one time, and it made complete sense to one of the ladies in the audience. She told me that, as a bank teller, she understood that even though she handles massive amounts of money daily, the money is not hers. It belongs to the bank. She is simply a manager.

I am a manager of the Lord's money. In reality, the money in my wallet is not mine; it is God's. Some Christians believe that ten percent of the money they receive is God's and the other ninety percent belongs exclusively to them. They are mistaken. It *all* belongs to God. We need to recognize His ownership in everything we have.

...for everything in heaven and earth is yours...wealth and honor come from you...(1 Chronicles 29:11b,12a).

"The silver is mine and the gold is mine," declares the Lord Almighty (Haggai 2:8).

For every animal of the forest is mine, and the cattle on a thousand hills (Psalms 50:10).

While LaVerne and I served as missionaries, I drove a van owned by the mission, and although I sensed responsibility for the van, I realized that it did not belong to me. Ultimately, it belonged to God. It was a good lesson in managing someone else's property that is similar to the responsibility God

REFLECTION
What is your responsibility as a "steward" of God's money (1 Corinthians 4:2)? Have you ever been entrusted with another person's money or possessions? How did you feel about those things?

has given us to manage the wealth He has given us. God has given us a responsibility as managers of His wealth. It all belongs to Him. We have to stop thinking like owners, and start thinking like managers.

We cannot serve God and money

Did you know God associates our ability to handle money with our ability to handle spiritual matters? One day Jesus made some amazing statements regarding this principle. *Whoever can be trusted with very little can also be trusted with much, and whoever is dishonest with very little will also be dishonest with much. So if you have not been trustworthy in handling worldly wealth, who will trust you with true riches? And if you have not been trustworthy with someone else's property, who will give you property of your own? No servant can serve two masters. Either he will hate the one and love the other, or he will be devoted to the one and despise the other. You cannot serve both God and Money (Luke 16:10-13).*

Money, in terms of true value, is a "little" thing. However, faithfulness in little things (money) indicates our faithfulness in big things (spiritual values). Jesus said that those who are not trustworthy in the use of their worldly wealth will be the same with spiritual things. Jesus said that we cannot serve two masters—God and materialism. It is impossible to hold allegiance to two masters at the same time.

Being surrounded with the world's riches may give us a false sense of security. Christians must not hold on too tightly to possessions because they have a way of deceiving us and demanding our hearts' loyalty. How we handle finances often is a reflection or indicator of our hearts. The Lord is very concerned with our use of finances because He knows that if He can trust us with finances, He can trust us with spiritual things.

REFLECTION
Why can't we serve both God and money?
How can money be like a "master" to us?

We should expect financial blessings

It amazes me to see how God constantly takes risks on His creation. When God created the angels, He took a risk. The archangel, Lucifer (Satan), tried to exalt himself above the Lord, so God had to throw him out of heaven (Isaiah 14:12-17). When God created mankind, giving us free wills, He took a risk.

Did you know that every time God blesses us financially, He is taking a risk? He takes a risk with you and me when He asks us to be stewards (managers) of His finances and material possessions, because we may begin to serve money instead of serving the true God. God, at times, blessed Israel with wealth as a sign that He was fulfilling His covenant. *But remember the Lord your God, for it is he who gives you the ability to produce wealth...(Deuteronomy 8:18).* We should expect financial blessings from the Lord. God wants us to be fruitful.

However, with the blessing of wealth, the Lord instructed His people to be careful so that they did not forget the Lord their God. God knows that our tendency is to allow money to be our God. We must remember that our lives do not consist in the abundance of the things that we possess...*Watch out! Be on your guard against all kinds of greed; a man's life does not consist in the abundance of his possessions (Luke 12:15).*

In the first of the Ten Commandments, the Lord commands us to "have no other gods before Him." The last commandment says we should not "covet what belongs to our neighbors." To *covet* means *to desire enviously that which belongs to another.* If we covet others' financial blessings, we are putting money ahead of God. Material possessions do not give life to us. Only a relationship with Jesus produces life! We must not allow material wealth to distract us from our heavenly calling.

REFLECTION

Why is God taking a risk by making us managers of His finances?
With financial blessing, what should we be careful of?

Is it better to be rich or poor?

Christians may fall into one of two camps when it comes to what they believe is God's perspective regarding a Christian's financial life-style—some may take the viewpoint that all Christians should be poor and others may take the viewpoint that all Christians should be rich.

Those who believe all Christians should be rich often believe financial wealth is a clear sign of God's blessing. However, God's "blessing" cannot *always* be equated with personal material gain. It involves so much more! God certainly wants to bless us financially. He wants to bless us in every way. *Dear friend, I pray that you may enjoy good health and that all may go well with you, even as your soul is getting along well (3 John 1:2).*

However, if we believe, like the Pharisees did, that great wealth is a *sign* of God's favor, we will look down on people who are poor. The Pharisees looked down on Jesus for being financially poor (Luke 16:14). But Jesus did not do the same. In fact, we see that the people of the church at Smyrna were destitute, yet Jesus said they were spiritually rich (Revelation 2:8-10). Although God wants to prosper us in every way, including financially, financial wealth does not necessarily mean we are blessed by God. The Laodicean Christians were a case in point. Scripture tells us they were wealthy, yet they were considered spiritually "wretched" (Revelation 3:17).

On the other hand, many wealthy people *are* blessed by God because they use their finances unselfishly. Job was a rich and godly man who did not allow his money to become his god (Genesis 13:2). Abraham also had great wealth and was very godly (Job 1). Before he had an encounter with Jesus, Zacchaeus, a wealthy tax collector, trusted his riches instead of trusting in the living God. But after he met Jesus, he gave back four times what he had taken from others (Luke 19:8).

In the other camp, and often in reaction to the very seductive power of money in our lives, some believers take the viewpoint that all Christians should be poor. They often have a fear of what money can do to them. They fear its corrupting influence and believe money will cause them to backslide. Some may have been wounded by financial scandals in the church and now reject any kind of wealth as having an evil influence.

Cutting through the smoke of the two opposing viewpoints, the truth is this: The Lord is not for or against money; it has no morality to Him. Money is amoral in and of itself. It is *what we do with it* and *our attitude toward it* that makes it moral or immoral. Money is not the root of evil like some people like to misquote in I Timothy 6:10.

In this scripture, the Lord warns us to beware of the pitfall of *loving* money. It is the *love* of money that is a root of all kinds of evil. *For the love of money is a root of all kinds of evil. Some people, eager for money, have wandered from the faith and pierced themselves with many griefs (1 Timothy 6:10).*

REFLECTION

Is money a sign of God's favor? Is money the root of all evil (1 Timothy 6:10)? Then what is the root of all evil?

We can be lovers of money, whether we have little or much. It depends on what we are placing our affections in. Rich or poor, if we begin to love money, it will lead us down the path of greed and cause much pain in our lives and in the lives of those around us.

DAY 6 Giving keeps us from materialism

Although God wants to bless us materially, it should not be our focus. *People who want to get rich fall into temptation and a trap and into many foolish and harmful desires that plunge men into ruin and destruction (1 Timothy 6:9).*

The Lord does not want us to have money on our minds all the time. Materialism is a preoccupation with material rather than spiritual things. Our primary focus should be on the kingdom of God, not on money. However, it does take money to expand the kingdom of God. We should not be a slave to money because God's purpose for money is for it to be a servant to us. Money is for purchasing the necessities of life and giving to those in need and to finance the spread of the kingdom of God. This bears repeating: The real purpose for receiving God's prosperity is to expand the kingdom of God.

Giving keeps us from materialism. Giving breaks the power of money to become an idol in our lives. God wants to bless us so we can sow into His kingdom and help the poor.

To be blessed financially simply means we have all that we need to meet the needs in our lives, and an abundance left over to give to others. The purpose for having a job and working should be for...*doing something useful with [our] his own hands, that [we] he may have something to share with those in need (Ephesians 4:28b).*

When we diligently work and faithfully give of our finances, the Bible teaches that God "will meet all our needs according to His glorious riches" (Philippians 4:19). He wants to meet our needs and enable us to meet the needs of others. God promises to take care of us. He wants to bless and prosper us! If you are a businessman, an employee, a student or a house-wife, the Lord desires to prosper you. Remember, God revealed Himself to Abraham as *El Shaddai*...the *God of more than enough.* He promised to bless Abraham abundantly, just as He desires to meet our needs and abundantly bless us in every way today. Giving really does keep us from getting materialistic.

REFLECTION
What can happen if our focus is on getting rich (1 Timothy 6:9)? What is the real purpose for receiving God's prosperity?

DAY 7

Give sacrificially, and your own needs will be met

In Luke 21, Jesus gives a lesson on how God evaluates giving. Jesus and His disciples were watching people putting their gifts into the temple treasury. The rich put in large amounts of money because they could easily spare it, but then a poor widow dropped two small coins in the treasury. She gave all she possibly could, and it required great personal sacrifice. Jesus remarked that the poor widow put in more than all the others because of the amount of sacrifice it required of her.

It is not the amount we give, but the sacrifice that is involved. When we give out of a heart of love and compassion for others, we will discover that God will take care of our own needs and more! As we give generously, God promises...*to make all grace abound to you, so that in all things at all times, having all that you need, you will abound in every good work...Now he who supplies seed to the sower and bread for food will also supply and increase your store of seed and will enlarge the harvest of your righteousness. You will be made rich in every way so that you can be generous on every occasion, and through us your generosity will result in thanksgiving to God (2 Corinthians 9:8,10-11).*

You can give either sparingly or generously. You are rewarded accordingly...*with the measure you use, it will be measured you (Matthew 7:2).* When you give sacrificially, God resupplies what you have given and increases your giving capacity. The more you give, the more you are blessed, and the more you can give. God wants to bless you financially so you have enough for yourself and enough to share with others.

REFLECTION
Recall some instances where you gave sacrificially and God took care of your needs.

Biblical Foundations

The
Tithe

Giving a portion of our income

The Lord gives us the responsibility to manage the resources He gives to us. He has set up a system to constantly remind us of His ownership in everything. This systematic way to give is a first step to allowing our resources to be used for God's kingdom. In the Old Testament, the Israelites were required to give one-tenth of all their income to the Lord. The Hebrew word for *tithe* means *a tenth part*. At the very heart of tithing is the idea that God owns everything. God was simply asking the Israelites to return what He first gave them. *Honor the Lord with your wealth, with the firstfruits of all your crops; then your barns will be filled to overflowing, and your vats will brim over with new wine (Proverbs 3:9-10).*

We honor God by giving Him the "firstfruits" or a portion of our income. It shows that we honor Him as the Lord of all our possessions. This tithe (10%) opens up a way for God to pour out His blessings on us. Every time we give our tithes, we are reminded that all of our money and earthly possessions belong to God. We are simply stewards responsible for what the Lord has given us. The word *tithe* is first mentioned in Genesis 14:18-20. *Then Melchizedek king of Salem brought out bread and wine. He was priest of God Most High, and he blessed Abram, saying, "Blessed be Abram by God Most High, Creator of heaven and earth. And blessed be God Most High, who delivered your enemies into your hand." Then Abram gave him a tenth of everything.*

Abraham gave Melchizedek a tithe before the Old Testament law had ever been written. Abraham was honoring the Lord and Melchizedek as the priest of the Most High God with ten percent of that which the Lord had given to him. He may have learned this principle from Abel who brought the firstborn of his flock to the Lord.

REFLECTION
Why does God require a portion of our income? What does the tithe symbolize?

At the end of every month I face a stack of bills that I need to pay. One of these bills is my bill to God. It is called a *tithe*, my "firstfruit." This tithe reminds me that everything I have belongs to Him. I have learned to enjoy returning this 10% to the Lord. After all, Jesus has given to me 100% of Himself through His death on the cross. I am eternally grateful!

Don't try to steal from God

In the 1992 riots in Los Angeles, California, looting took place in many stores and businesses. A young man was asked by a reporter what he had stolen. He said, "I stole Christian tapes because I am a Christian." You might think that sounds ridiculous. Yet, in a similar way, there are many Christians who are stealing from God by keeping for themselves that which really belongs to the Lord—the tithe.

In Old Testament history, some of the Israelites were robbing God by selfishly holding onto money that belonged to God. They were required to give at least one-tenth of the livestock, the land's produce and their income to the Lord. In addition they were required to bring other offerings in the form of sacrifices or free-will offerings. But God says they were holding back. *"Will a man rob God? Yet you have robbed Me! But you say, 'In what way have we robbed You?' In tithes and offerings. You are cursed with a curse, for you have robbed Me, even this whole nation. Bring all the tithes into the storehouse, that there may be food in My house, and try Me now in this," says the Lord of hosts, "If I will not open for you the windows of heaven and pour out for you such blessing that there will not be room enough to receive it. And I will rebuke the devourer for your sakes, so that he will not destroy the fruit of your ground, nor shall the vine fail to bear fruit for you in the field," says the Lord of hosts (Malachi 3:8-11 NKJ).*

When the people asked God how they were robbing Him, He responded clearly, "In tithes and offerings." Notice, He not only tells us to bring "tithes," but also "offerings." We'll talk more about offerings in Chapter 3.

Many of God's people today are robbing God in this same way. The Lord has promised us that if we obey Him and bring all of our tithes into the storehouse, He will open the windows of heaven, pour out a blessing on us, and "rebuke the devourer." Many people are struggling financially because the devil has been robbing and devouring them. The enemy has not been rebuked by the Lord, because they are not paying tithes into the storehouse.

We are blessed as God rebukes the devourer when we tithe. However, our primary motivation for tithing should not be to get something back from God. Our primary motivation for tithing is obedience—to God and His Word.

I've known some people who have said that when they initially began to tithe, the enemy attacked them, and they found themselves worse off financially than ever before. The enemy may test us when we obey the Word of God. When Jesus was baptized, the heavens opened, and the Lord said, "This is my beloved Son in whom I am well pleased." During the next forty days of His life, Jesus was tested by the enemy. Tests will always come; however, if we hold on, we will receive the blessing that comes from obedience. God's promises always prove to be true!

When I was a missionary, the enemy tested me in the area of tithing. "You gave your entire life to God," he told me, "how could the Lord expect you to give back a tithe from the small amount of money you are receiving?" By the grace of God, I refused the enemy's lies and began to tithe even the small amount the Lord had provided for us. The Lord blessed us over and over again in a supernatural way as we served in the mission field. God is faithful. He honors His Word.

The tithe is a bill to God

DAY 3

The tithe is a numerical expression reminding us that all we have belongs to God. Some years ago, I was reading the book of Malachi and was convicted by the Lord in the area of tithing. I checked my bank ledger. I had a whole list of bills. In fact, one of the bills I was delinquent in paying was my bill to God. Every month, my bill to God grew. I was not paying my tithe because I thought I did not have enough money to pay it.

One day, I made a decision to obey God. When I received my next paycheck, I paid all of my tithes to God. Some time later, I realized something supernatural had happened after I had taken this step of obedience. Our money seemed to last longer! The Lord began to provide for us financially, often in supernatural ways. It didn't happen overnight, but God began to bless us in a new way, and the devourer was rebuked.

Some people say, "I can't afford to tithe." The truth is—they cannot afford to withhold the tithe. A tithe is money set apart for God. If we don't give it to God, the devourer will consume it. Let's read again what God says in His Word about rebuking the devourer when we give tithes and offerings into His storehouse. *And I will rebuke the devourer for your sakes, so that he will not destroy the fruit of your ground, nor shall the vine fail to bear fruit for you in the field...(Malachi 3:11 NKJ).*

The word *devour* in the original Hebrew text means *to eat, burn up or consume.* During the days of Malachi, God's people were experiencing famine, scarcity, unseasonable weather, and insects that ate up the fruits of the earth. According to the above scripture, the enemy will devour our blessings when we choose to not obey God's principles. When we walk out from under the umbrella of protection of obedience to the Word of God concerning tithing, it gives the enemy a legal right to devour our blessings.

According to Webster's dictionary, *a tithe is 10% of one's income paid as a tax to the church.* When you pay your taxes to the government, do you *feel* like paying it? Do we have to *feel* like paying our tithe back to God? Of course not. Whether or not we *feel* like tithing is not the issue. We need to tithe in *obedience* to Him.

Imagine going to the bank and paying off a loan or a mortgage. How does the bank teller respond when we pay? Does she pat us on the back and tell us how much she

REFLECTION
Who will devour our money if we do not tithe?
How have you experienced the blessings of God by tithing?

appreciates it that we came to pay our bill? No, and neither should we expect God to pat us on the back when we tithe. We are not doing God any great favor when we tithe. It belongs to Him anyway. It is our responsibility to tithe, and we do it out of obedience.

Giving systematically

The Lord wants us to learn to give systematically just like the believers were encouraged to do in 1 Corinthians 16:2. *On the first day of every week, each one of you should set aside a sum of money in keeping with his income, saving it up, so that when I come no collections will have to be made.*

Some believers claim to "follow the Spirit" as to when they will tithe. That's like calling your electric company and saying, "I'm not sure if I will pay my bill this month. Maybe I'll pay it next month. I'm just going to follow the Spirit." If you did not pay, you would get your electric service disconnected. We should always follow the Holy Spirit within the framework of the Word of God. The Word of God teaches us to tithe systematically as an act of obedience, not just when we feel like it.

Imagine giving your employer a phone call and telling him, "I will come to work when I think the Spirit is prompting me to come." Guess what would happen? You would probably lose your job! The same principle applies to giving to the Lord in a systematic way. Yes, we should follow the Spirit in our giving that is over and above our regular tithes. However, our God is a God of order and discipline. He instructs us to give tithes systematically so we do not have to "catch up on our giving" because we didn't give on a consistent basis.

Some believers say, "I think I'll pray about tithing." That's a bit like praying about whether or not we should read the Bible regularly or whether or not we should be part of a local church. These principles are clear in the Word of God, just like tithing.

I have been asked, "Should we tithe on the net (wages I receive after my taxes are paid) or the gross (wages I receive before the taxes are paid)?" When we pay your taxes to the government, do we pay taxes on the net or on the gross? We pay on whatever we have received (the gross amount). As Christians, we should desire to give everything we possibly can back to God because of what Jesus Christ has done for us. Remember, tithing is not an option. It is an act of obedience to God. It is a privilege to return to God what is already His.

REFLECTION
Why is it important to give systematically?
What does it teach us?

Attitudes toward tithing

Sometimes Christians believe that tithing is simply an Old Testament doctrine. Dr. Bill Hamon says, "One divine principle in biblical interpretation is that whatever was established in the Old Testament remains proper as a principle or practice unless the New Testament does away with it. For instance, tithing was established in the Old Testament, but since nothing is stated in the New Testament that abolishes it, then it is still a proper practice for Christians."[1]

Jesus confirms the Old Testament principle of tithing in the New Testament. However, He does not want us to tithe with the attitude of the scribes and Pharisees in Matthew 23:23. The Lord sharply rebuked their attitudes about tithing. *Woe to you, teachers of the law and Pharisees, you hypocrites! You give a tenth of your spices-mint, dill and cummin. But you have neglected the more important matters of the law—justice, mercy and faithfulness. You should have practiced the latter, without neglecting the former.*

The religious Pharisees appeared spiritual and godly, but they were not in right standing with God. They tithed right down to the last tiny mint leaf, but their hearts were selfish and hard.

The Lord affirms that we should tithe today, but He is concerned about our attitudes as we give to Him. In the Old Testament, God's people tithed because the law required it. Since the New Testament, we should tithe because the Lord has changed our hearts. It is a privilege to return the tithe back to Him. We tithe as an act of love for our God and also out of a heart of generosity and love for others.

Let's imagine you ask me to come to live in your house. The only stipulation is that, monthly, I need to pay 10% of all the things you provide for me. You fill the refrigerator, put gas in the car and provide all of my living expenses. It would be ridiculous for me to begin to think that everything is mine. Nothing is mine,

REFLECTION

What attitude do you have when you give to God? What are you learning about the tithe?

because it belongs to you. Giving ten percent reminds me that it all belongs to you. That's what tithing is all about. The Lord's purpose for tithing is to remind us that everything we have belongs to Him.

[1]Dr. Bill Hamon, *Prophets And The Prophetic Movement*, (Shippensburg, PA: Destiny Image Publishers, 1990), p. 197.

God will provide

When we recognize that everything we are and have belongs to the Lord, it will be easier for us to trust the Lord to provide for us when we tithe. Even if we do not have much, God will provide when we give to Him. Giving has a way of releasing our finances. Let's learn again from the widow who gave a mite (a fraction of a penny) into the temple treasury. She sacrificially gave more than the many others who threw in large amounts because she gave all she had. *Calling his disciples to him, Jesus said, "I tell you the truth, this poor widow has put more into the treasury than all the others. They all gave out of their wealth; but she, out of her poverty, put in everything—all she had to live on" (Mark 12:43-44).*

God knows our hearts and honors our obedience in tithing. It might seem like a sacrifice, but in the long run, it helps us to become masters over our money instead of becoming a master to it.

What about those who just cannot tithe? For example, if your spouse is unsaved, you may find yourself in a dilemma. He or she may not want you to tithe. If a spouse does not agree to tithe, you cannot give something that is not yours to give. If you are the co-owner of a restaurant, you don't tithe on all the money that you take in because half of it belongs to the other owner. In the same way, you should not give away your family's money against your spouse's wishes.

Here are a few recommendations: Appeal to your spouse in faith. For example, you could say, "Could I give some money to the church this week on a regular basis?" Pray and allow the Holy Spirit to work in his or her heart. Ask the Lord for personal money you could tithe. Perhaps you occasionally make some extra money at a side job—you could tithe on that personal money. Remember, God looks at our hearts and honors our obedience no matter how small our tithe may be.

REFLECTION
Explain how the poor widow put more in the temple treasury than the rich. Do you believe God will meet your needs as you tithe?

Where should the tithe go?

Where should we give our tithes? As we learned before, Malachi 3:10a says, *Bring the whole tithe into the storehouse, that there may be food in my house....*

According to this scripture, all the tithes should be placed into the storehouse. The storehouse is where spiritual food is kept to bless those who lead us, feed us and equip us for ministry. In the Old Testament, the Levites and the priests were responsible to spiritually lead and feed God's people. The tithe paid for the work of those who were set apart for the purpose of ministry to the Lord and to His people. The Levites were dependent upon the faithfulness of God's people in giving tithes to support them. *I give to the Levites all the tithes in Israel as their inheritance in return for the work they do while serving at the Tent of Meeting (Numbers 18:21).*

Since the Old Testament is a "type and a shadow" of the New Testament, the principle of where to tithe applies in the New Testament. We should tithe to the storehouse of our spiritual leaders because they are called by the Lord to minister the Word and encourage us.

Church leaders are called to "equip the saints for the work of ministry" (Ephesians 4:11-12). They need to be financially supported so that they have enough time to devote to prayer and ministering the Word of God to the saints under their care. In Acts 6:4, the leadership of the early church knew their responsibility was to single-mindedly "give their attention to prayer and the ministry of the Word."

REFLECTION
Who should be financed from the "storehouse"?

A man once told me, "I give my tithes whenever I see a need." This man did not know it, but he was not giving a tithe, he was giving an offering. An *offering* is anything we give over and above the 10%. Tithes are the first 10% of our income given into the storehouse to provide finances to help support those who are equipping and giving spiritual leadership to the saints in the local church. *The elders who direct the affairs of the church well are worthy of double honor, especially those whose work is preaching and teaching (1 Timothy 5:17).* The word *honor* refers to *giving financially* to those who labor among us in spiritual oversight, prayer, teaching and training in the Word of God.

Now that we know what a tithe is and where it should be given, let's examine the importance of giving both tithes *and* offerings in the next chapter.

CHAPTER 3

Give Both Tithes and Offerings

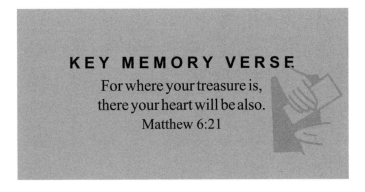

KEY MEMORY VERSE

For where your treasure is,
there your heart will be also.
Matthew 6:21

The difference between a tithe and an offering

As we just learned in the last chapter, we need to take care of the needs of those who give us spiritual oversight by giving them our tithes. As we give our tithes into the storehouse (the local church where we are fed spiritually), we are taking care of the needs of our spiritual leaders. Galatians 6:6 says that those who are taught God's Word should help provide material support for the instructors. *Anyone who receives instruction in the word must share all good things with his instructor.*

Verses 7-10 of the same chapter go on to say that if we refuse to give support to these faithful leaders, we are sowing selfishness and reaping destruction. But if we give to these leaders, it is part of "doing good to all people, especially to those who belong to the family of believers." These faithful leaders in our church are worthy of our support, and we are right in supporting them (1 Corinthians 9:14; 3 John 6-8; 1 Timothy 5:18).

Our tithe to our local church should be our first priority for giving. This kind of giving is only a place to start, however. We need to give over and beyond our tithes to many worthy causes. "Offerings" are monies given above ten percent. We should give offerings to many places and causes both within and outside our local church.

As Christians, we have a responsibility to give to the poor and needy, especially those within the church. We are encouraged to show a concern for the poor. Jesus expected that His people would give generously to the poor. Proverbs 28:27 says, *He who gives to the poor will lack nothing....*

REFLECTION
What is your responsibility to the one(s) who teaches you (Galatians 6:6)? In your own words, explain the difference between a tithe and an offering.

In addition, we should also give to those who feed us spiritually from places other than our local church—perhaps through a book, a TV ministry, or another para-church ministry. These are some of the many, many places where we can give our offerings.

I have heard various radio Bible teachers say, "Do not send me your tithes; send me your offerings—that which is over and above ten percent. Your tithe belongs to your local church." I believe those

Bible teachers are properly discerning the scriptures concerning the difference between tithes and offerings.

In conclusion, our tithe should go into the storehouse of the local church, and our offerings should go where we, cheerfully, voluntarily and generously, believe God is leading us to give.

Heart and money matters

We usually place our finances in areas that are the most important in our lives. Matthew 6:21 says that wherever we place our money, that's where our hearts will be. *For where your treasure is, there your heart will be also.*

Riches can demand the total loyalty of one's heart. That's why God tells us we must decide in our hearts to serve God and not money in Matthew 6:19-24. People who place their money in stocks, immediately check out the stock market page whenever they receive their daily newspaper. Why? Because that is where their interests lie; they are concerned about where their finances are placed. Where we give both our tithes and our offerings shows what we place high value on.

Since the Lord has called us to faithfully support our local church, it is important that we are placing our tithes in the storehouse of the local church. We encourage God's people involved in our church to faithfully tithe in obedience to the Lord, because when we tithe to our local church, our hearts are with God's people and with those who serve among us. Consequently, tithing is an issue of the heart—not a law. If we have decided within our hearts to give to our local church and its leadership, we will joyfully give our tithes to the storehouse in our church.

REFLECTION
What does Matthew 6:21 tell us about our hearts?
Why is tithing an issue of the heart and not the law?

Giving a tithe shows we trust our leadership. When we are not willing to give a tithe, we begin, even without knowing it, to sow seeds of distrust. Tithing is a test in trust; trust in our God and trust in those the Lord has placed in spiritual leadership over our lives.

Tithing—a test in trust

Let's take a moment to review. A tithe, as we learned, is 10% of our income—a reminder that all we have belongs to the Lord. Offerings are gifts we give to the Lord, His people and His work that is over and above the 10% tithe. In the same way that unforgiveness opens the door for the tormenter to bring depression and confusion into people's lives (Matthew 18:34-35), robbing God of the tithe to the storehouse opens the door for the enemy to rob us. We must trust God and support His work with our tithes, according to Malachi 3:10b. *"Test me in this," says the Lord....*

God is speaking of faith and trust when He tells us to tithe to the storehouse, the place where provisions were kept for the local Levites who were serving God's people. God's people gave to the storehouse in faith because they trusted the Levites to distribute the money properly. Today the same principle of trust applies: the tithe goes into the storehouse of the local church to meet the needs of spiritual leadership who equip and encourage the church. God's plan is for those who spiritually feed and lead us to be supported by tithes. *If we have sown spiritual seed among you, is it too much if we reap a material harvest from you? If others have this right of support from you, shouldn't we have it all the more? But we did not use this right. On the contrary, we put up with anything rather than hinder the gospel of Christ. Don't you know that those who work in the temple get their food from the temple, and those who serve at the altar share in what is offered on the altar? In the same way, the Lord has commanded that those who preach the gospel should receive their living from the gospel (1 Corinthians 9:11-14).*

REFLECTION
How is trust a part of giving your tithe?

You may wonder, "Where should the pastor (senior elder) of a church tithe?" In some churches, the pastor tithes into the storehouse of those who give him oversight encouragement and accountability. This is often a team of spiritual leaders in the pastor's denomination or fellowship of churches.

A question to ask: Are you tithing?

Malachi 3:8-12 asks the question, "Have you robbed God?" Our response usually is, "Who, me? How could I ever do that?" And then the Lord tells us how—"in tithes and offerings." Are you tithing? If not, according to the scriptures, you're robbing God. Today is the day to repent before the Lord and begin to tithe in obedience to the Word of God.

Perhaps you are disobeying the Lord by withholding tithes and offerings because you had a bad experience in the past. A young person, who is the product of a broken home, may not want to get married because of witnessing a bad marriage between his parents while growing up. However, marriage is still a wonderful plan of God. Even though you may have had bad experiences in churches where money was misused, it is still the Lord's plan for us to give our tithes and offerings into the local church. We need to press on...*forgetting what is behind and straining toward what is ahead, I press on...(Philippians 3:13-14a).*

REFLECTION
If we are robbing God, what should we do?
If we have had bad past experiences, what does Philippians 3:13-14 encourage us to do?

The Lord will honor you by rebuking the devourer and opening the windows of heaven. You will also find a new sense of trust in your God and trust in those He has placed in your life who serve you in areas of spiritual leadership.

Are you tithing to the storehouse?

After God tells His people in Malachi 3 where to tithe—to the storehouse, He promises to pour out a huge blessing if they are obedient...*and see if I will not throw open the floodgates of heaven and pour out so much blessing that you will not have room enough for it (Malachi 3:10b).*

God wants to bless us, but we should tithe where He recommends—the storehouse. Are we tithing, but not to our church family? That would be like buying a hamburger at McDonalds and paying for it at Burger King! In the Old Testament, when the tithe was withheld from the storehouse, the Levites could not fulfill their role. The same is true today. In some parts of the body of Christ, pastors and other spiritual leaders are struggling financially because the tithes are being withheld in the congregations in which they serve. Consequently, they do not have enough time to effectively serve the people of God because of needing to support themselves through "tent-making" (business). The enemy can devour God's people through disobedience. Of course, some leaders, like Paul the apostle, do choose to make "tents," and this is acceptable and encouraged if the Lord has led them to do so.

What are some examples of giving our tithes to other places besides the storehouse (our church)? Giving our tithes to para-church ministries, missionaries, evangelists or other ministries are a few examples. Although there are many missionaries, evangelists, and other Christian workers who are reputable men and women of God and need our financial support, according to my understanding of the scriptures, they should be supported through *offerings*, not through *tithes*. If we give our tithes to them, it can open the door for unbelief and lack of trust to come into our local church family. The tithe should be placed into the storehouse of our local church to be distributed to support those who give us spiritual protection and equip us to minister.

To clarify a common "tithing misunderstanding," David Wilkerson, founder of Teen Challenge and pastor of the Times Square Church in New York City, wrote in his newsletter some time back, "Concerning my statement recently about sending your tithe to our ministry, I received about 35 letters, many from pastors, lovingly reminding me that tithes belong in the local church. I totally agree. I should have clarified my statement. We have quite a number of people on our readers' list who do not attend church, sometimes because their church is shut down or they do not have a suitable church home...Believers really need to find a church home and support it. Until then, however, often my messages are the only spiritual food some people have. Overwhelmingly, those who support this ministry are faithful to support their local church, and they give us over and above their tithes."

> **REFLECTION**
> *What does God promise if we tithe to the storehouse (Malachi 3:10)? What is wrong with designating where we want our tithe to go within the local church?*

Another question to ask is this: are you tithing to the storehouse, but designating your tithe instead of freely giving it like the people in

Malachi 3? Some believers are very willing to tithe to the storehouse, but try to control the church by withholding the tithe or a portion of the tithe, or by designating it to be used for certain things only. When we pay our taxes, we do not tell our government to spend some of the taxes on the army and another portion of our taxes to remodel a room or buy new furniture for our president or prime minister. Likewise, in our local church, when we give our tithes to the storehouse, we must trust our spiritual leadership to distribute it in a way that honors the Lord.

Excuses to rob God

There are many reasons why Christians rob God of the tithes and offerings. One reason is simply **ignorance**. *Truly, these times of ignorance God overlooked, but now commands all men everywhere to repent (Acts 17:30 NKJ).* If you have been ignorant about this truth, you can repent (turn around) and begin to obey this spiritual truth. We serve a merciful God. He desires to bless us as we obey Him.

Some of God's people do not tithe and give offerings in direct **disobedience to the Word of God**. If we claim to know the Lord, but are not willing to obey His Word, the scriptures tell us that we are liars. We need to repent and obey the living God. *The man who says, "I know him," but does not do what he commands is a liar, and the truth is not in him (1 John 2:4).*

Another reason that some believers do not give tithes and offerings is because of **personal debt**. The Bible says in Galatians 6:7 that...*a man reaps what he sows.* The lack of giving could be part of the reason for being in debt. I read about a Christian businessman who was in debt ten times greater than his yearly income. Yet he obeyed the Lord and began to tithe and give sacrificial offerings. Within the next few years, he saw his entire financial situation turn around. God prospered him and he became a pastor of a church. The Lord began to use him to teach the truths of the Word of God regarding tithing and giving offerings and giving to hundreds of people in his community.

If you find yourself in debt, seek counsel from a trusted Christian who has wisdom in these matters. You may need to develop new habits in sound financial management. Many years ago, a Christian friend showed me how to set up a budget. Managing finances with a budget has been a real blessing to me. A budget will not control our finances, but it will give us a picture of where they are going and what the needs are.

Some people do not give tithes and offerings because they think they are **too poor**. The Lord is not concerned about the amount of money we give; He is more concerned about our attitude toward giving. Even if we have little, we can give in proportion to what God has given us. If we give nothing, we are like a farmer who eats his seed and does not have a crop for the following year. If we eat our seed (using our tithe for something other than what it was intended for), we are hindering the blessing of God in our lives.

This brings us to still another reason why many of God's people withhold their tithes and offerings. They simply **do not trust their leadership**. If we do not trust our leadership in our local church to handle the tithes we give, then we need to ask the Lord for grace to trust our spiritual leaders. If we still cannot trust them, we may be in the wrong church. 1 Corinthians 12:18 tells us that God places us in the body as He wills. It is not the church of *our* choice; it is the church of *His* choice. We need to be among a group of believers where there is a sense of faith and trust in the leadership that God has placed there.

REFLECTION
Have you ever used any of the excuses listed here for not tithing? Explain.

DAY 7

Receive new freedom

If you are not tithing and giving offerings, I exhort you to start today by tithing to your church. You will receive a new freedom in your life and relationship with others in the local church family in which you serve. Secondly, ask God to bless you in a way that you can give generous offerings to ministries of integrity. There are many ministries that are worthy of our gifts and offerings; however, be sure to check out where you give. The Lord holds us responsible to give offerings to reputable ministries. Do not be afraid to do your homework before giving.

Remember, tithing is a test in trust—a trust in our God who has promised to rebuke the devourer and open the windows of heaven. And it is also a trust in the spiritual leaders in our local church, as we tithe into the storehouse. The Lord desires to set us free to joyfully give our tithes and offerings to Him. And He desires to bless us as His children who obey His voice.

John 8:36 tells us, *so if the Son sets you free, you will be free indeed.*

May the Lord bless you and open the windows of heaven for you as you walk in obedience to these spiritual truths. In the last chapter of this book, we will look at how to manage the money and material wealth with which the Lord has blessed us.

REFLECTION

Describe ways you have been set free to give—in both your tithes and offerings.

Biblical Foundations

CHAPTER 4

How to Manage the Finances God Has Given

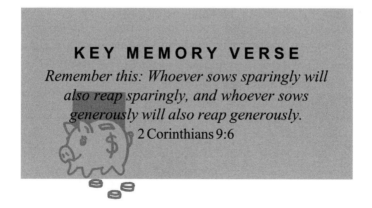

KEY MEMORY VERSE

Remember this: Whoever sows sparingly will also reap sparingly, and whoever sows generously will also reap generously.
2 Corinthians 9:6

Faithful with what we have

The finances and possessions the Lord has given to us belong to Him. We are simply managers of that which He has given.

1 Corinthians 4:2 says...*Now it is required that those who have been given a trust must prove faithful.*

We are entrusted with God's money. So then, the finances and possessions that we have should be used to honor God and build His kingdom. We must faithfully use what God has given us.

The Lord also wants us to be content with the finances that He's given to us. Paul said ...*I have learned to be content whatever the circumstances (Philippians 4:11).*

To be content means *to be free from complaining.* There are times that our family has lived with very little and other times we have been abundantly blessed. Either way, God has called us to be content and triumphantly live above our changing circumstances.

People today often want their needs gratified immediately, so they go deeply into debt to buy the things they think they cannot do without. This is a financial mistake and breeds discontent.

It is also a mistake to want to get rich quick instead of paying the price faithfully, obeying God, day by day. This kind of "lottery thinking" or "waiting until I get a big break" is really "poverty thinking." If we focus on a distant chance that may come, we will be hindered from moving forward financially today. Financial advancement comes to those who apply God's principles on a consistent, long-term basis (Hebrews 6:12).

Remember the parable of the talents (Matthew 25:14-30)? One man had five talents and was faithful with the five. Another man had two. The Lord knew he was responsible enough to handle two talents. The third man only received one. Why did God give him just one talent? That was all he could handle at that point. God knows what we can handle. When we are faithful with what He has given, He blesses us with more.

REFLECTION
What is the first requirement of a good manager according to 1 Corinthians 4:2? Why are "get-rich-quick" schemes detrimental?

Provide for our families

The Lord wants to bless us financially in order to meet the needs of our family. *If anyone does not provide for his relatives, and especially for his immediate family, he has denied the faith and is worse than an unbeliever (1 Timothy 5:8).*

For even when we were with you, we gave you this rule: If a man will not work, he shall not eat (2 Thessalonians 3:10).

A man gave his life to the Lord and was convinced he should spend all of his time witnessing. He spent his time out on the beach, witnessing every day, while his family was nearly starving. He believed that somehow God would be obligated to provide for his family, since he was so busy doing "God's work." When his Christian friends challenged him to take care of his family, he became defensive. "Wasn't he telling others about Jesus? What could be more important than that?" The truth was that he was disobeying the Word of God. God was not telling him to be out witnessing when his family was not being properly taken care of. If the Lord calls you as a missionary who "lives by faith," it is important not to do it at the expense of your family. I have been privileged to proclaim the gospel and train Christian leaders in various parts of the world. However, my first responsibility is for my own family. Any Christian who refuses to provide for his own family has denied the faith and is worse than an unbeliever.

Some people say to me, "I want to be involved in a full-time ministry, supported by the church." This can be a noble desire, however, the truth is that everyone is involved in a full-time ministry. If you are working at a secular job, you are in full-time ministry. You're called to minister at your job.

So why do we work? Is it to have money to buy expensive material possessions? Not at all. The Bible tells us we work to give to him who is in need (Ephesians 4:28). It starts with providing for our own families and helping those whom the Lord has placed around us.

It is a blessing to be able to work. Don't wait for the perfect job. Start somewhere and God will give you the perfect job in the future as you are faithful in the opportunity He has given you today.

REFLECTION
What does 1 Timothy 5:8 teach us about taking care of our families? Examine your life; are you motivated to work for the right reasons?

Investing our Master's wealth

How do we invest our Master's wealth to see His kingdom built in a way that will honor Him the most? First of all, we invest the Lord's money to evangelize the world. Remember the story of the prodigal son? His father gave half of his wealth to the son who promptly wasted it. That young man eventually came back to his father, but it cost his father half of his fortune. In other words, the father used all of that money to see one soul saved. The Bible tells us in Mark 8:36 that we cannot put a price-tag on a soul. *What good is it for a man to gain the whole world, yet forfeit his soul? Or what can a man give in exchange for his soul?*

In our church, we encourage every Christian to support a missionary somewhere in the world. Why? According to the Bible, wherever we place our money, that is where our heart will be (Matthew 6:21). And since God loves the world so much, our missionary support keeps our hearts at the same place as our God's—reaching the world. The money we give to support a missionary of our choice is not taken from our tithe. It is taken from the 90%—an offering. Anything that is given above the 10% is an offering to the Lord. By investing our offerings into someone like a missionary, we are helping to invest the Lord's money to evangelize the world.

A practical way to invest our wealth is to invest in stocks or bonds or mutual funds that give a financial increase. Like the man in the Parable of the Talents who invested wisely, we will receive an increase with wise investments. This increase can help expand the kingdom of God.

REFLECTION
How can you gain the whole world at the expense of your soul (Mark 8:36)? In what ways are you investing your wealth for the kingdom of God?

Money and relationships

We can also use the Lord's money to honor Him and build His kingdom by using it to build relationships. Jesus told the story of a manager who was being fired. His boss said, "Clean up your accounts; you're going to be fired." So the manager quickly found a man who owed the boss eight hundred gallons of oil. He said to the man, "Pay me for four hundred gallons." He found someone else who owed a thousand bushels of wheat and said, "Just rip up the original bill and pay for eight hundred bushels." The boss of the corporation came back and saw what the manager had done. Instead of being angry, the Bible says in Luke 16:8-9, *The master commended the dishonest manager because he had acted shrewdly. For the people of this world are more shrewd in dealing with their own kind than are the people of the light. I tell you, use worldly wealth to gain friends for yourselves, so that when it is gone, you will be welcomed into eternal dwellings.*

The manager was commended by his master because he was acting very shrewdly. He used his master's finances to build relationships. He knew he was going to be without a job and needed relationships with other people. Although this manager was dishonest, and Jesus never condones dishonesty, there is a truth we can learn from this story. Jesus says that the people in the world are shrewder than God's children. In other words, many non-Christians have learned to use finances to build relationships, while in the church, we have often not understood this important principle.

We need to use our finances to build relationships. Take someone out for a meal, and you will be building a relationship that will last for eternity. A young man once told me that as a little boy he met an older Christian man who bought him an ice cream cone. That thirty-five cent ice cream cone opened him up to God through his relationship with this Christian man. Do you know why? The man was using his money to build relationships.

Baking a cake for your neighbor will help to build a relationship. Inviting someone into your home for hospitality or for a meal is using the money the Lord has entrusted to you to build relationships with people that will last for eternity. The Bible says in Matthew 5:16...*let your light shine before men, that they may see your good deeds and praise your Father in heaven.*

Our actions speak louder than our words. The way we use our money can cause people in the world around us to fall in love with Jesus Christ and live eternally with Him. Remember, Jesus Christ lives in us (Galatians 2:20). People often learn to trust Jesus as they learn to trust us.

REFLECTION
Describe some times you have used your money to build a relationship. Repeat Matthew 5:16 aloud while changing the word "your" to "my." Make it your prayer.

Helping the poor is like investing money in God's bank

In both the New and the Old Testament, the Lord requires us to give to help those who are poor. James 1:27 says, *Religion that God our Father accepts as pure and faultless is this: to look after orphans and widows in their distress and to keep oneself from being polluted by the world.*

Deuteronomy 15:7-8 tells us, *If there is a poor man among your brothers...do not be hardhearted or tightfisted toward your poor brother. Rather be openhanded and freely lend him whatever he needs.*

Jesus said, *For I was hungry and you gave me something to eat, I was thirsty and you gave me something to drink, I was a stranger and you invited me in, I needed clothes and you clothed me, I was sick and you looked after me, I was in prison and you came to visit me. (Matthew 25:35-36).*

Giving to the poor
Matthew 6:1-4; Matthew 19:21
Luke 12:33;14:12-14,16-24;
18:22; Matthew 25:31-46

And then He said, a few verses later, *"...whatever you did for one of the least of these brothers of mine, you did for me."* In other words, when we help someone who is hurting because we love Jesus Christ, we are doing it unto Jesus.

I believe we will stand before God and He will say, "Remember the time you invited Me into your home?" or "Remember the time you helped Me when I was struggling financially?" Every time we invite someone into our home or help someone because of Jesus, we are doing it to Him.

If the Lord has blessed us financially, it is for the purpose of blessing those around us. *He who has pity on the poor lends to the Lord, and He will pay back what he has given (Proverbs 19:17 NKJ).*

According to the Bible, when we give to someone who is poor, we are placing the money in God's bank—the greatest bank in the whole world. If God tells you to give someone a certain amount of money, you are literally investing that money in the Lord's bank. The Lord will pay you back with His blessing when you invest money in His bank by giving to those who are poor.

REFLECTION
List some of our responsibilities to the poor.

Give freely and willingly to meet needs in the kingdom

The Lord also wants to bless us so we can meet needs in the body of Christ. 2 Corinthians 8:14 tells us, *At the present time your plenty will supply what they need, so that in turn their plenty will supply what you need. Then there will be equality.*

In other words, when one person has an abundance, he will supply the lack that someone else has. It reminds me of a balance scale. If my side of the scale is too heavy, I take some of the weight off my side and place it on your side of the scale. If you have extra, you give to someone else so they can be blessed by your abundance. If they have extra finances and you are going through a financial struggle, they can give to you so that you also may have what you need.

There are enough resources in the body of Christ to meet every need. I am not talking about a type of communism. Communism coerces people and forces "equality" on people under its influence. People should never be forced to give. In the kingdom of God, the Holy Spirit gives the Lord's people a desire to give to serve those who have a need in the body of Christ both in our communities, and in the mission field.

As we give, the Lord wants us to have proper attitudes and motives. 2 Corinthians 9:7 gives us a few biblical attitudes to consider as we give. *Each man should give what he has decided in his heart to give, not reluctantly or under compulsion, for God loves a cheerful giver.*

First of all, let's give cheerfully. I know of one church in the state of Texas, USA where the people are so excited about giving that they cheer and clap every time there is an offering given.

REFLECTION
What is the difference between God's equality and communism's way? How has it been a joy for you to give?

God has called us to give freely and willingly. Matthew 10:8b says...*freely you have received, freely give.* We also should not give grudgingly or because we have to. We need to give because we want to.

You may ask, "How much should I give"? When we go to a meeting of believers at our local church and they take a special offering, the Lord will give us a sense of peace so we can know how much we should give. The more we grow in the Lord and give, the more we grow in faith. Again, we don't give grudgingly or because we have to, but we give because it is a joy to give back to God that which is His already.

Give and it will be given

A friend of mine, a new Christian, was serving in the military. One day his friend borrowed money from him and did not pay him back. My friend struggled with unforgiveness, until he read this scripture in Luke 6:33-35. *And if you do good to those who are good to you, what credit is that to you? Even "sinners" do that. And if you lend to those from whom you expect repayment, what credit is that to you? Even "sinners" lend to "sinners," expecting to be repaid in full. But love your enemies, do good to them, and lend to them without expecting to get anything back. Then your reward will be great, and you will be sons of the Most High, because he is kind to the ungrateful and wicked.* When we give or lend money to others, it must be in faith. Whether or not it is returned to us, we must strive to keep our attitudes pure and continue to love, even our "enemies."

God has called us to give in faith. Luke 6:38 says, *Give, and it will be given to you. A good measure, pressed down, shaken together and running over, will be poured into your lap. For with the measure you use, it will be measured to you*

As we give, God says He wants to bless us by giving back to us the same measure we give to others. He is the One who is responsible to bless us. Although our motivation for giving must always be out of our love for God, the Lord desires to bless us when we give in obedience to Him. Many do not receive God's financial blessings because they have not experienced their faith and do not expect to receive God's abundance.

God also calls us to give liberally. 2 Corinthians 9:6 says, *Remember this: Whoever sows sparingly will also reap sparingly, and whoever sows generously will also reap generously.*

Let's give to others just as Jesus has been so faithful to give to us. It is, however, important to check out where we give. A pastor friend confided in me that his church had given thousands of dollars to a man in another nation, only to find out that this man was embezzling money from the church for his own personal use. Of course they stopped giving to the man. We need to be sure that we are giving to reputable Christian ministries. It is often good to give to those with whom we have a close personal relationship. We can trust them because we know them and see genuine spiritual fruit in their lives.

And finally, the Lord's desire is that we prosper. 2 Corinthians 8:9 says, *For you know the grace of our Lord Jesus Christ, that though he was rich, yet for your sakes he became poor, so that you through his poverty might become rich.*

REFLECTION
According to 2 Corinthians 9:6, how should we give?

Jesus Christ took the curse of poverty for us. He wants us to be blessed spiritually, relationally, physically, mentally, and financially. But remember, when He blesses us, He takes a risk. We may choose to trust in our financial riches instead of trusting in the living God. He desires to bless us so that we can bless those around us. May the Lord bless you as you fulfill your responsibility as a good manager (steward) of the finances He has entrusted to you.

We Are Managers of God's Money

1. God loves a cheerful giver

a. God wants to bless us financially (John 3:16, Genesis 17).

b. Giving should not be done grudgingly (2 Corinthians 9:7).

c. One out of ten verses in the New Testament addresses this subject. Our attitude toward money is often revealing of our relationship with God.

2. We are managers only

a. God owns our possessions; we are managers.

1 Corinthians 4:1-2,7

Ex: Bank teller handles money daily that belongs to the bank.

Missionaries used a vehicle that belonged to the mission, but were given responsibility for it.

b. God's ownership

1 Chronicles 29:11,12; Haggai 2:8; Psalms 50:10

3. We cannot serve God and money

a. God associates our ability to handle money with our ability to handle spiritual matters (Luke 16:10-13).

b. Holding too tightly to possessions deceives us and demands our heart's loyalty. We cannot serve both God and money.

4. We should expect financial blessings

a. God blessed Israel with wealth as a sign of fulfilling His covenant (Deuteronomy 8:18). We should expect financial blessing.

b. When God blesses us financially He takes a risk that we may start serving money rather than God (Luke 12:15).

5. Is it better to be rich or poor?

a. Although God wants to bless us financially (3 John 1:2), money is not always a sign of God's favor, or we would look down on the poor:

Ex: The people at the church in Smyrna were destitute, but Jesus said they were spiritually rich (Revelation 2:8-10). In contrast, the Laodicean Christians were wealthy yet spiritually wretched (Revelation 3:17).

b. Many people are blessed by God because they use their finances unselfishly.

c. People who fear that money will corrupt them often think it is better to be poor.

d. Money is amoral; it is what we do with it that makes it moral or immoral. The *love* of money is "a root of all kinds of evil." 1 Timothy 6:10

6. Giving keeps us from materialism

a. God wants to bless us, but it should not be our focus. 1 Timothy 6:9

b. The real purpose for receiving God's prosperity is to expand the kingdom.

c. When we are blessed financially, we can sow into God's kingdom and help the poor (Ephesians 4:28).

d. God will meet all our needs "according to His glorious riches" (Philippians 4:19).

7. If we give sacrificially, our own needs will be met

a. It is not the amount we give, but the sacrifices involved and heart attitude.

Ex: Poor widow gives two small coins in temple treasury. Luke 21

b. When we give generously, God promises to take care of our needs and more (2 Corinthians 9:8,10-11).

c. Giving sparingly or generously, we are rewarded accordingly (Matthew 7:2).

The Tithe

1. Giving a portion of our income

a. God set up a system to remind us of His ownership in everything—the tithe.

b. The Israelites were required to give one-tenth of all income to the Lord (Proverbs 3:9-10).

c. Abraham gave Melchizedek a tithe before the Old Testament law had been written (Genesis 14:18-20).

2. Don't try to steal from God

a. The Israelites were robbing God by holding back the tithe. Malachi 3:8-11

b. Today, people rob God the same way. God promises to "rebuke the devourer" when we tithe.

3. The tithe is a bill to God

a. We cannot afford to withhold the tithe or the devourer will consume it (Malachi 3:11).

b. A tithe is 10% of one's income paid as a tax to the church according to Webster's Dictionary. Do we always *feel* like tithing? Maybe not, but it is a bill to God just like we pay our electric bill or food bill.

4. Giving systematically

a. New Testament believers were encouraged to give systematically (1 Corinthians 16:2).

b. Tithing is an act of obedience to God, not an option.

5. Attitudes toward tithing

a. The scribes and Pharisees appeared godly and tithed right down to the last mint leaf, but their hearts were hard. Matthew 23:23

b. When we tithe, we must do it not because it is required but because it is an act of love for God and others.

6. God will provide

a. When we recognize that everything we have belongs to God, it is easier for us to trust the Lord to provide for us when we tithe.

b. Giving has a way of releasing our finances. It helps us to become masters over our money instead of being a master to it (Mark 12:43-44).

7. Where should the tithe go?

a. Malachi 3:10a says we should bring our tithes to the storehouse. The storehouse is where spiritual food is kept to bless those who lead and equip the body of Christ for ministry.

b. The Levites were those set aside to lead God's people. They were dependent on the people's tithes (Numbers 18:21).

c. Tithing supports those giving spiritual leadership to the saints in the local church (1 Timothy 5:17).

Give Both Tithes and Offerings

1. The difference between a tithe and an offering

a. The tithe helps provide support for our spiritual leaders (Galatians 6:6). If we refuse to give tithes, we are sowing selfishness (Galatians 6:7-10).

b. When we give over and beyond our tithes, we are giving an offering. We are responsible to give offerings to the poor and needy (Proverbs 28:27).

2. Heart and money matters

a. Our hearts will be where we place our money. Matthew 6:21

b. When we tithe to our church, our hearts are with God's people and those who serve us. Giving a tithe shows we trust our leadership.

3. Tithing—a test in trust

a. Trust God (Malachi 3:10b) and support His work with your tithe.

b. Those who spiritually feed us should be supported by tithes. 1 Corinthians 9:11-14

4. A question to ask: Are you tithing?

a. Some people will not tithe because they had a bad past experience.

b. We need to press on...(Philippians 3:13-14) and find a new sense of trust in God and those in leadership.

5. Are you tithing to the storehouse?

   a. When we are obedient to tithe to the storehouse, the Lord promises a blessing (Malachi 3:10b).

   b. Some people give their tithes to para-church organizations, missionaries, evangelists, etc. However, the tithe should go to the local church and offerings should go to these other places.

   c. Designating where we want our tithe to go in the church or withholding our tithe may be a type of control. We must give freely and trust our leadership.

6. Excuses to rob God

   a. Ignorance: They have not been taught of its importance today (Acts 17:30).

   b. Disobedience to God's Word: They are in direct disobedience (1 John 2:4).

   c. Personal debt: Their lack of giving may be a reason for the debt (Galatians 6:7).

   d. They think they are too poor.

   e. They do not trust their leadership.

7. Receive new freedom

   a. If you are not tithing, start today by tithing to your church.

   b. In addition, ask the Lord to bless you so you can give offerings.

   c. Be set free to joyfully give. You are free indeed (John 8:36).

How to Manage the Finances God Has Given

1. **Faithful with what we have**
   a. We are entrusted with God's money (1 Corinthians 4:2).
   b. We should be content (free from complaining) with what we have (Philippians 4:11)
   c. Get-rich-quick schemes are really "poverty thinking." Financial advancement comes to those who apply God's principles on a consistent long-term basis (Hebrews 6:12).

2. **Provide for our families**
   a. God wants to bless us so we can provide for our family. 1 Timothy 5:8; 2 Thessalonians 3:10
   b. Whether we are in full-time ministry or hold a secular job, we are called to be ministers of Christ.
   c. We work so we have money for our families and have money to give to others (Ephesians 4:28).

3. **Investing our Master's wealth**
   a. We should use our money to evangelize the world. We cannot put a price tag on a soul (Mark 8:36).
   b. Giving our offerings to support a missionary is a way to reach the world.

4. **Money and relationships**
   a. We can use our finances to build relationships. Luke 16:8-9
   b. Our actions speak louder than words (Matthew 5:16). Bake a cake for your neighbor. Invite someone into your home.

5. **Helping the poor is investing money in God's bank**
   a. The Lord requires us to give to the poor.
   James 1:27; Deuteronomy 15:7-8; Matthew 25:35-36
   b. If God has blessed us financially, it is for the purpose of blessing the poor around us (Proverbs 19:17). The Lord will repay our investment from His "bank."

6. **Give freely and willingly to meet needs in the kingdom**
   a. God wants to bless us so we can meet needs in the body of Christ, supplying our abundance to those who lack.
   2 Corinthians 8:14
   b. God loves a cheerful giver (2 Corinthians 9:7).

7. **Give and it will be given**
   a. When we give or lend money to others, it must be in faith. Whether or not it is returned to us, we must strive to keep our attitudes pure and continue to love, even our "enemies." Luke 6:33-35
   b. God wants to give back to us in the measure we have given. Luke 6:38
   c. God wants us to give liberally (2 Corinthians 9:6).
   d. God wants us to prosper (2 Corinthians 8:9).

Chapter 1
We are Managers of God's Money
Journaling space for reflection questions

DAY 1 *Why does God want to bless us financially? What should be our attitude in giving?*

DAY 2 *What is your responsibility as a "steward" of God's money (1 Corinthians 4:2)? Have you ever been entrusted with another person's money or possessions? How did you feel about those things?*

DAY 3 *Why can't we serve both God and money? How can money be like a "master" to us?*

Why is God taking a risk by making us managers of His finances? With financial blessing, what should we be careful of?

Is money a sign of God's favor? Is money the root of all evil (1 Timothy 6:10)? Then what is the root of all evil?

What can happen if our focus is on getting rich (1 Timothy 6:9)? What is the real purpose for receiving God's prosperity?

Recall some instances where you gave sacrificially and God took care of your needs.

Chapter 2
The Tithe
Journaling space for reflection questions

DAY 1

Why does God require a portion of our income? What does the tithe symbolize?

DAY 2

What does God promise in Malachi 3, if we bring our tithes into the "storehouse"?

DAY 3

Who will devour our money if we do not tithe? How have you experienced the blessings of God by tithing?

DAY 4 *Why is it important to give systematically? What does it teach us?*

DAY 5 *What attitude do you have when you give to God? What are you learning about the tithe?*

DAY 6 *Explain how the poor widow put more in the temple treasury than the rich. Do you believe God will meet your needs as you tithe?*

DAY 7 *Who should be financed from the "storehouse"?*

God's Perspective on Finances

Chapter 3
Give Both Tithes and Offerings
Journaling space for reflection questions

DAY 1 *What is your responsibility to the one(s) who teaches you (Galatians 6:6)? In your own words, explain the difference between a tithe and an offering.*

DAY 2 *What does Matthew 6:21 tell us about our hearts? Why is tithing an issue of the heart and not the law?*

DAY 3 *How is trust a part of giving your tithe?*

DAY 4 *If we are robbing God, what should we do? If we have had bad past experiences, what does Philippians 3:13-14 encourage us to do?*

DAY 5 *What does God promise if we tithe to the storehouse (Malachi 3:10)? What is wrong with designating where we want our tithe to go within the local church?*

DAY 6 *Have you ever used any of the excuses listed here for not tithing? Explain.*

DAY 7 *Describe ways you have been set free to give—in both your tithes and offerings.*

Chapter 4
How to Manage the Finances
God Has Given
Journaling space for reflection questions

DAY 1

What is the first requirement of a good manager according to 1 Corinthians 4:2? Why are "get-rich-quick" schemes detrimental?

DAY 2

What does 1 Timothy 5:8 teach us about taking care of our families? Examine your life; are you motivated to work for the right reasons?

DAY 3

How can you gain the whole world at the expense of your soul (Mark 8:36)? In what ways are you investing your wealth for the kingdom of God?

DAY 4 *Describe some times you have used your money to build a relationship. Repeat Matthew 5:16 aloud while changing the word "your" to "my." Make it your prayer.*

DAY 5 *List some of our responsibilities to the poor.*

DAY 6 *What is the difference between God's equality and communism's way? How has it been a joy for you to give?*

DAY 7 *According to 2 Corinthians 9:6, how should we give?*

Daily Devotional Extra Days

If you are using this book as a daily devotional, you will notice there are 28 days in this study. Depending on the month, you may need the three extra days' studies given here.

How Important Is It?

DAY 29

Write down two verses on tithing and two verses on offerings.
Explain the difference between the tithe and offerings.
Since so much of the Bible has to do with finances and steward-ship, how important do you think this matter is in life?

What Changes Can I Make?

DAY 30

Read Matthew 6:33. Besides money, of what other things are we stewards for God's use? What about your "time"?
What changes can you make in your life-style to be more effective in building the kingdom of God?

What Have You Learned?

DAY 31

Write out a verse that has especially blessed you in this book about finances. How has it changed you?

Coordinates with this series!

Biblical Foundations for Children

Creative learning experiences for ages 4-12, patterned after the *Biblical Foundation Series*, with truths in each lesson. Takes kids on the first steps in their Christian walk by teaching them how to build solid foundations in their young lives. by Jane Nicholas, 176 pages: $17.95   ISBN:1-886973-35-0

Other books by Larry Kreider

House to House

The church is waking up to the simple, successful house to house strategy practiced by the New Testament church. *House to House* documents how God called a small fellowship of believers to become a house to house movement. During the past years, DOVE Christian Fellowship Int'l has grown into a family of cell-based churches and house churches networking throughout the world. by Larry Kreider, 206 pages: $8.95   ISBN: 1-880828-81-2

The Cry for Spiritual Fathers & Mothers

Returning to the biblical truth of spiritual parenting so believers are not left fatherless and disconnected. How loving, seasoned spiritual fathers and mothers help spiritual children reach their full potential in Christ. by Larry Kreider, 186 pages: $11.95 ISBN: 1-886973-42-3

The Biblical Role of Elders for Today's Church

New Testament leadership principles for equipping elders. What elders' qualifications and responsibilities are, how they are chosen, how elders are called to be armor bearers, spiritual fathers and mothers, resolving conflicts, and more. *by Larry Kreider, Ron Myer, Steve Prokopchak, and Brian Sauder.* $12.99 ISBN: 1-886973-62-8

Check our Web site: www.dcfi.org

Spiritual Fathering & Mothering Seminar

Practical preparation for believers who want to have and become spiritual parents. Includes a manual and the book *The Cry For Spiritual Fathers & Mothers.*

Effective Small Group Ministry Seminar

Developing strategy for successful cell groups. For cell leaders and pastors. Includes a *House To House* book and a seminar manual.

Youth Cell Ministry Seminar

Learn the values behind youth cells so cell ministry does not become just another program at your church. For adult and teen leaders!

New House Church Networks Seminar

Learn how new house churches (micro-churches) are started, kept from pitfalls, and work with the rest of the body of Christ.

Elder's Training Seminar

Based on New Testament leadership principles, this seminar will equip elders to provide protection, direction and correction in the local church. Includes *The Biblical Role of Elders in Today's Church* book and a manual.

Church Planting Clinic

Designed to help you formulate a successful strategy for cell-based church planting. For those involved in church planting and those considering it. Includes a *Helping You Build Cell Churches* Manual.

Counseling Basics Seminar
for Small Group Leaders

This seminar takes you through the basics of counseling, specifically in small group ministry. Includes a comprehensive manual.

Fivefold Ministry Seminar

A seminar designed to release healthy, effective fivefold ministry in the local church. Includes a *Helping You Build Cell Churches* Manual.

Marriage Mentoring Training Seminar

Trains church leaders and mature believers to help prepare engaged couples for a strong marriage foundation by using the mentoring format of *Called Together.* Includes a *Called Together* Manual.

Seminars held at various locations throughout the US and Canada. For complete brochures and upcoming dates:

Call 1-800-848-5892
www.dcfi.org   email: info@dcfi.org